# First World War
### and Army of Occupation
# War Diary
### France, Belgium and Germany

GUARDS DIVISION
1 Guards Brigade
Headquarters
1 January 1917 - 31 January 1917

WO95/1213/4

The Naval & Military Press Ltd
www.nmarchive.com
Published in association with The National Archives

Published by

The Naval & Military Press Ltd

Unit 10 Ridgewood Industrial Park,

Uckfield, East Sussex,

TN22 5QE England

Tel: +44 (0) 1825 749494

www.naval-military-press.com

www.nmarchive.com

*This diary has been reprinted in facsimile from the original. Any imperfections are inevitably reproduced and the quality may fall short of modern type and cartographic standards.*

© **Crown Copyright**
**Images reproduced by permission of The National Archives, London, England, 2015.**

# Contents

| Document type | Place/Title | Date From | Date To |
|---|---|---|---|
| Heading | WO95/1213 Jan 1917 | | |
| Heading | O i/c AG's Office Base. | | |
| Heading | HQ 1 Gds Bde. Vol 19. | | |
| War Diary | Combles | 01/01/1917 | 02/01/1917 |
| War Diary | Combles To Meaulte | 03/01/1917 | 03/01/1917 |
| War Diary | Meaulte | 04/01/1917 | 09/01/1917 |
| War Diary | Meaulte To Ville | 10/01/1917 | 10/01/1917 |
| War Diary | Ville | 11/01/1917 | 20/01/1917 |
| War Diary | Meaulte | 21/01/1917 | 24/01/1917 |
| War Diary | Ville | 25/01/1917 | 25/01/1917 |
| War Diary | Ville To Billon Farm | 26/01/1917 | 26/01/1917 |
| War Diary | Billon | 27/01/1917 | 31/01/1917 |
| Miscellaneous | Daily Intelligence Report-1st Guards Bde., 8 a.m. Jan: 1st to 8 a.m. Jan: 2nd. | 01/01/1917 | 01/01/1917 |
| Miscellaneous | Daily Intelligence Report-1st Guards Brigade. 8 a.m. Jan: 2nd to 8 a.m. Jan: 3rd. | 02/01/1917 | 02/01/1917 |
| Operation(al) Order(s) | Warning Order. Guards Division Order No. 104. | 02/01/1916 | 02/01/1916 |
| Operation(al) Order(s) | Warning Order 1st Guards Brigade Order No. 96 | 03/01/1917 | 03/01/1917 |
| Miscellaneous | Handing Over Notes. | 31/12/1916 | 31/12/1916 |
| Miscellaneous | Amended Instructions No. 1 for Right Group. | 27/12/1916 | 27/12/1916 |
| Miscellaneous | Amended Instructions No. 2 for Right Group. | 28/12/1916 | 28/12/1916 |
| Operation(al) Order(s) | Guards Division Order No. 105. | 08/01/1917 | 08/01/1917 |
| Operation(al) Order(s) | Amendment To Guards Division Order No. 104 | 07/01/1917 | 07/01/1917 |
| Miscellaneous | March Table To Be Attached To Guards Division Order No. 104. | | |
| Operation(al) Order(s) | Warning Order (2) Guards Division Order No. 104. | 06/01/1917 | 06/01/1917 |
| Miscellaneous | Provisional March Table. | | |
| Operation(al) Order(s) | 1st Guards Brigade Order No. 96. | 08/01/1917 | 08/01/1917 |
| Miscellaneous | March Table | | |
| Operation(al) Order(s) | 1st Guards Brigade Order No. 97. | 09/01/1917 | 09/01/1917 |
| Miscellaneous | 1st G.B. No. 98/2. | 28/01/1917 | 28/01/1917 |
| Miscellaneous | 1st Guards Bde. No. 1225. | 17/01/1917 | 17/01/1917 |
| Miscellaneous | Normal Attack Formation. | | |
| Miscellaneous | G.D. No. 2660/G | 13/01/1917 | 13/01/1917 |
| Miscellaneous | 1st Guards Bde. No. 1288 | 19/01/1917 | 19/01/1917 |
| Operation(al) Order(s) | Guards Division Order No. 106. | 21/01/1917 | 21/01/1917 |
| Miscellaneous | Movement Of Battalions Etc. During relief. Appendix "A". | | |
| Miscellaneous | Distribution Of Guards Brigades Etc. On Completion Of Relief. Appendix "B". | | |
| Miscellaneous | G.D. No. 2696/5/G. | 22/01/1917 | 22/01/1917 |
| Miscellaneous | | | |
| Operation(al) Order(s) | 1st Guards Brigade Order No. 98/1. | 23/01/1917 | 23/01/1917 |
| Miscellaneous | March Table "A"/1 Giving Routes, Times Of Starting For Movements Ordered In 1st Guards Brigade Order No. 98. | | |
| Miscellaneous | Fatigues to be Handed Over to 2nd Guards Brigade. Table "B". | | |
| Miscellaneous | Relief of Decauville Fatigue at Briqueterie Camp (Map ref. A.4.b.5.2.) Table "C". | | |

| | | | |
|---|---|---|---|
| Miscellaneous | Fatigues to be taken over from 3rd Guards Brigade. Table "D". | | |
| Operation(al) Order(s) | 1st Guards Brigade Order No. 98. | 21/01/1917 | 21/01/1917 |
| Miscellaneous | Movements Of Battalions Etc., During Relief. Table"A". | | |
| Operation(al) Order(s) | 1st Guards Brigade Order No. 99. | 28/01/1917 | 28/01/1917 |
| Operation(al) Order(s) | Amendment to 1st Guards Brigade Order No. 99. | 29/01/1917 | 29/01/1917 |

WO 95
12.13
Jan 1917

On His Majesty's Service.

To the Adjt. Office
Keane

NOI Edo Bible
Vol 19

**Army Form C. 2118.**

# WAR DIARY or INTELLIGENCE SUMMARY
*(Erase heading not required.)*

Instructions regarding War Diaries and Intelligence Summaries are contained in F. S. Regs., Part II. and the Staff Manual respectively. Title Pages will be prepared in manuscript.

Headquarters 1st Guards Brigade

| Place | Date | Hour | Summary of Events and Information | Remarks and references to Appendices |
|---|---|---|---|---|
| COMBLES | Jan 1 | | Casualties Nil. | |
| | | | Relief of the Div. started in accordance with 1st Gds. Bde. Order No. 95 & (1st) Div. Bat. | App 288 288/A |
| | | | neighbourhood of SAILLY CHATEAU & CHURCH settled 10.3 | |
| | | | Gone of day - settled 4.2 " | |
| | | | The enemy have apparently spotted the duckboards leading from CHATEAU | |
| | | | to Right Bⁿ. a prisoner from 120th Regiment captured by 2nd Coldstream | 9/g Intelligence |
| | | | during night. | |
| Jan 2 | | Casualties. 1st Colds. Gds. O.R. killed 1. | 2/9 291 |
| | | | 2nd Colds. Gds. O.R. wounded 1. | |
| | | | 1st Scots Gds. O.R. wounded 1. (accidentally) | |
| | | | The enemy shelled the Reserve line & left Bⁿ. heavily in order to | |
| | | | silence their guns the support of the heavy artillery & counter battery group | |
| | | | were called for. | 292 Intelligence |

# WAR DIARY or INTELLIGENCE SUMMARY

Army Form C. 2118.

| Place | Date | Hour | Summary of Events and Information | Remarks and references to Appendices |
|---|---|---|---|---|
| COMBLES to MEAULTE | Jan 3rd | 12 noon | Casualties - 2nd Coldstream Gds. O.R. killed 1. wounded 1. | |
| | | 8 a.m. | 2nd Div Order No. 104 received - further Div. would take over another portion of the line on Jan 7th. 1st Gds Bde order No 95 issued | APP 293 293/A |
| | | 6.30 p.m. | Relief of Bde by 61st Bde complete. The day was also a quiet one - a bombardment which was to have been carried out by the heavy artillery was postponed. For notes on the line handed over see General instructions for the night front see | APP 294 APP 295 |
| MERICOURT | Jan 4th | 5.30 pm | The Brigadier held a conference of C.O.'s at Bde H.Q. at 5.30 p.m. | |
| | Jan 5 | 10.5 am | The Brigadier inspected billets of 2/Coldstream Gds. | |
| | Jan 6 | 11 am | Divisional Conference at 11 am at 3/Gds Bde H.Q. at VILLE. The Divl General outlined the programme of the Division for the next few weeks. | |
| | | 5.20 pm | Lecture by O.C. No 9 Squadron R.F.C. at MERICOURT. All officers and Platoon S/Os of the Brigade attended. The subject of lecture - Contact Patrols was explained. | |

# WAR DIARY or INTELLIGENCE SUMMARY

Army Form C. 2118.

| Place | Date | Hour | Summary of Events and Information | Remarks and references to Appendices |
|---|---|---|---|---|
| MEAULTE | Jan 7 | 2 pm | The Brigadier held a Conference of Commanding Officers at Bde. H.Q. to discuss Bde. Sn. Order No 104 giving the organization of Brigades and a general outline of the defence scheme. Training schemes were also discussed. Particulars of the Div. Conference held at Div. H.Q. in the previous day were also discussed. | |
| | Jan 8 | 10 am | Capt Redwith-Smith D.S.O. went to the Div. H.Q. to take up the duties of G.S.O.I. temporarily to the Divn. in Brigadier's absence | 297 |
| | | 9.30 am | A few days furlough Leave was granted for Officers in the Bde. who had not already permitted leave through absence. The number of Officers attending today was 244. The day was fine & cool. | |
| | 8.9. | 8 am | Bde. Op. Order No 75 issued for move of Bde - S. Recd 4523 : | 296 |
| | | 4 pm | Bombing course for officers completed. The day was cloudy but here no rain. | |
| | | | Notes on Movement Orders 210 received. Was did not relieve places to move but considerably increased the fatigues. | |
| | | 7 pm | Capture was of Fatigue Parties issued to Units. RBd H.B. No 358/1. | |
| | 9th | 10 am | The Brigadier saw No. 1 + 2 Cos. 2/ Grenadier Gds. at Company Drill. | |
| | | 11 am | Inspected 2/ Grenadier Gds. Battln. | |
| | | 11.30 am | Inspected 2/ Coldstream Gds. Battln. G. | |
| | | 4 pm | Mrs Asquith visited Offrs of Guards Gdo. at MEAULTE | |

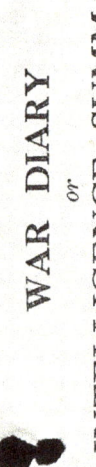

# WAR DIARY or INTELLIGENCE SUMMARY

Army Form C. 2118.

| Place | Date | Hour | Summary of Events and Information | Remarks and references to Appendices |
|---|---|---|---|---|
| MEAULTE to VILL E. | Jan 10 | | The Bde moved to new billets as per Bde Orders No 96 & 97. | App 297 & 298. |
| VILLE | Jan 11 | | Drill parades for three men of Bdes not on fatigues were carried out. The Brigadier had laid great stress on the carrying out of steady drill by Battns every day. A new training ground at VILLE STATION - & the improvement of billets began again. | |
| " | Jan 12 | 10 am 11 am | Brigadier inspected billets of 2 2 d Gloucesters " " " 2 nd B n Devonshire Regt. | |

# WAR DIARY or INTELLIGENCE SUMMARY

Army Form C. 2118.

| Place | Date | Hour | Summary of Events and Information | Remarks and references to Appendices |
|---|---|---|---|---|
| VILLE | 13th | 3 p | The Major General visited Bde H.Q. Later the Brigadier inspected Baths at MAULTE | |
| | 14th | | Heard Sunday Stories. All Officers Received Pour le 17th 6mm, afer Order No 2 AM 25/1/3 T.S. Bde Bombing Course WR Col. Jensen cond 11.30 p.m. each Ge W. R.E. N.C.O instructed around to Lewkors Battles in revetting. | X17 |
| | 15th | | | |
| | 16th | 10 am | The Brigadier inspected Bte R.Q. Transport. | |
| | | 11 am | Visited 17th Bn Lord Dewar MERICOURT | |
| | | 2 pm | And also the 2nd Gordon cr Pd. at Bde Drill, Bayonet Fighting and Grenade Throwing | |
| | | 3 pm | Visited the 17th ranges MAULTE | |
| | | | 17th Bayford bind Lieutenant R. returned from today's leave. | |
| | 17th | | Normal attack formation for Bde before wires returned & sent note Office No 225 and in conjunction with GR No 2660/9 of 13 Inst | 300 |
| | | | T.M. Battery returned to billets in MAULTE from T.M. Course. Weather becoming warmer & fine day. | |

**Army Form C. 2118.**

# WAR DIARY
## or
## INTELLIGENCE SUMMARY
*(Erase heading not required.)*

Instructions regarding War Diaries and Intelligence Summaries are contained in F. S. Regs., Part II. and the Staff Manual respectively. Title Pages will be prepared in manuscript.

| Place | Date | Hour | Summary of Events and Information | Remarks and references to Appendices |
|---|---|---|---|---|
| VILLE | 18/1/17 | 3pm | 2 Cold. Stream Guards taken over billets at MORBECOURT No=32 from 1st Welsh Gds. | |
| | | 10.30 am | Brigadier attended Conference of Brin H.Q. MOISLAINS, pursuant to H.Q. Conference secret order Appx. Q.9. No 3685/1/9 a.115. This appx No=38. shown in attached. From A Coy Standing Orders on Defence amended as G.S. 443 received and distributed. | 301 |
| | | | Weather dull apart, heavy showers in the evening. Training as usual. | |
| | 19th | 9am | 1st Bn Coldstream arrived. | |
| | | 12am | Brigadier visited & inspected 9 Gds and 2nd Battns on the Brewing of MOISLAINS and ordered training of Christmas N.C.Os. | |
| | | | ATTACK SCHEME under appx No=289 read to Units, to occur on 21st | |
| | | 3 pm | Field News Egg book, hot chocolate | |
| | | 3.30pm | Brigadier visited reserve trenches. | |
| | | | Freezing. | |
| | 20th | 9am | Corps Commander visited 2nd Coldstream of the and 1st Welsh Gds. H.R.H. accompanied by Brigadier. | |
| | | 10am | Brigadier inspected 1st Bn Irish Guards Billets and training. | |
| | | 11am | Brigadier visited 5 Coldstream for heads of training candidates for Commissions. | |
| | | 3pm | | |
| | | | Weather very cold, hard frost. | |

# WAR DIARY or INTELLIGENCE SUMMARY

Army Form C. 2118.

| Place | Date | Hour | Summary of Events and Information | Remarks and references to Appendices |
|---|---|---|---|---|
| 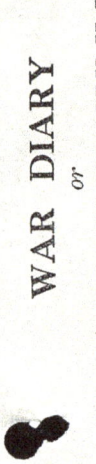 | 21st | 9am | Bn. Sim. Order No.136 received. See hour of the Bn. to form Corps Reserve & 93rd Reserve in Billets FARM area. | |
| | | 5pm | Since Parade as usual. 1st Glo'ste Bde No.93 received & noted. Warning order for Horse Shows 24th & 25th shown in attached file. Fine, no frost. | 302 |
| | 22 | 10am | Inspection of gas helmets & and of the Brigade in Citadel Zed P.1800 under AA.KINNEAR F.A. | |
| | | | Inspn. of men of Bn. finished 3. | |
| | | | Report on Bn. front received in this office for serial work at 5.8th order 5/2m N.2 | |
| | | 10.30 | Prac. Lecture by Col. FOULKES @ CITADEL (R.215) 12 junior officers attended. | |
| | | 2.30 | The Brigadier inspected parties from each Bn. with full marching kit in order to arrive at some standard equipment for the Bde. | |
| | 23rd | -- | Weather fine, hard frost. | |
| | | 10 a.m. | The Brigadier inspected Canadian N.C.O. attached & 2 Lts. transfer and posted for a/c of April. | |
| | | 3 pm | Orders to have issued under No.8/Bde Order 93/1 also re left of Platoon etc shown in attached | 303 |
| | | | Weather fine. Hard frost. | |
| | 24 | 10.30 am | Brigadier inspected Canadian N.C.Os attached to 1st Gloucester Regt 3rd Gloucesters etc at April. | |
| | | 9 a.m. | 2 Lt Cottgreave Glos Regt Proc'd for Potter Comp to arrived 12 noon. | |

# WAR DIARY or INTELLIGENCE SUMMARY

Army Form C. 2118.

| Place | Date | Hour | Summary of Events and Information | Remarks and references to Appendices |
|---|---|---|---|---|
| MEAULTE VILLE | 25th | | 2 Gunners for 7 & 8 Battalion Bn. left for MEAULTE for FRIEZ from 2nd Bidon Camp 107 supervision | |
| | | 2pm | 3rd Bidon roof - 14 personnel Camp 107. Stores of Rations from Horses Wire 34th Bn was laid up with "Stomatitis" weather very mild hard frost | |
| NULLE to BILLON FARM | 26th | 9am | Bde. M.G. Coy. and T.M. Batty move to Camp 16 BILLON FARM. | |
| | | 11:30 | Bdt. H.Q. move to BILLON FARM. Weather very cold. Hard frost. Mud fine. | |
| BILLON | 27th | 10am | 1st Irish Gds. have Mentioned and move to Camp 107 BILLON FM transport moved south and stores from each Battn. 2 Grenadiers Front Batt. in FRIEZ FARM. Casualties 2 killed 5 wounded 5 slight | |
| | | | Coys of 1 & 2 Coldm Bngds. Pont Battn. in FRIEZ FARM. | |
| | | 3pm | Coys of 1 Coldm & 2 Coldm relieved M.G. Coy. and T.M. Battery, Camp 16, and gave through attack practise Scheme south of Ypres - Tyne | |
| | | 4pm | Companies bivouacs two M.G. B3 - Coldstream Gds. Grenadiers Rifle 1 wounded Weather fine and frost | |
| | 28th | | Casualties March 2nd Grenadier Gds. (Coy FM) 1 wounded (slight) | (307) |
| | | | 1st G.B. Order No. 99 issued for relief of Batth. at Friez thirds ordered for... | |

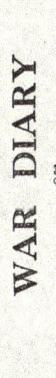

Weather fine, hard frost.

# WAR DIARY
## or
## INTELLIGENCE SUMMARY

Army Form C. 2118.

| Place | Date | Hour | Summary of Events and Information | Remarks and references to Appendices |
|---|---|---|---|---|
| BULFORD | 29th | | Bgn 3 Bttn Trench fate relieve 2nd Grenadier Gds at PRIEZ FARM. Brigadier inspects 2 Irish Guards Bn. M.Gs. at Training. Lieut Col L Boyd of 3rd Gren Gds. officer No 99 stood shown to attached hereunder Command later to 2nd G.G. Officer No 99 stood shown to attached hereunder. Brigadier holds Tour of Camps to circulate with camp improvement scheme issued under G.R.O. No 583/5/a of 18/1/17. — | 303 |
| | 30 | Morn | Brigadier received pm some Conveners' Butcher in respect of sub Committees. Brigadier inspects Butcher in respect of sub Committees. Brigadier inspects Bulford in Grenadier Grenade Camps. Training carried on as usual. Lists of field stores from Divn. & 5 GI on Q form have been submitted previously. 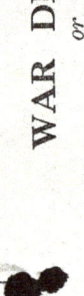 Weather snow showers thawed — thaw cold. |  |
| | 31 | | Brigadier inspects Training. | |
| | | 2.15pm | Cold damp snow attack scheme 2/IR LIFE and 3 Grenadier Gds resolve. Weather fine, hard frost. | |

2/2/17

J. S. Jeffreys
Brigadier General
Command 2 Guards Bde

Daily Intelligence Report - 1st Guards Bde.,

8 A.M. Jan: 1st to 8 A.M. Jan: 2nd.

## OPERATIONS.

Relief. 1st Bn. Coldstream Guards relieved 2nd Bn. Coldstream Guards in the left sub-sector. Relief complete 8-10 P.M.

Patrols. Two patrols were sent out during the night by the left Battalion. Nothing to report - Enemy very quiet except opposite right Battalion.

Snipers. Inactive on both sides.

Aircraft. Nil.

## HOSTILE ARTILLERY.

Activity normal. Enemy appeared to be registering on our front line U 14 7 and U 14 6 from the direction of LE TRANSLOY.

Hostile Battery observed about U 3 a 1.0 - This Battery began firing on two Green Lights being sent up and ceased on a series of Red, Green, Red, Red.

## INTELLIGENCE.

Considerable Machine Gun and Rifle Fire at every 'Stand To' opposite right Battalion - Otherwise very quiet.

Enemy reported to be holding his line strongly and working hard at it opposite right Battalion. It is suggested that a Strong Point is being made about U 14 b 9.4. Two Machine Guns are suspected here.

Less movement than usual behind the lines is reported, but various small parties were seen in the direction of ROCQUIGNY and BUS.

No Train movements reported.

Signals. Flash lamp was seen on BUS Church.

Captain,

Intelligence Officer, 1st Guards Bde.,

Intelligence Report - 1st Guards Brigade.

8 A.M. Jan: 2nd - 8 A.M. Jan: 3rd.

## OPERATIONS.

*Relief.* 1st Bn. Irish Guards was relieved in the right sub-sector by the 7th Bn. Som. L. I. Relief complete 9-45 P.M.

*Patrols.* Patrol went out from right of left Battn. at 9 P.M. They report no movement or noise in the enemy's front line.

*Aircraft.* Two hostile planes came over our lines at 3-30 P.M.: they quickly returned.

*Sniping.* Left Battalion claim two victims. Reports indicate that the enemy are becoming more careful of exposing themselves, and even at long ranges always move about at the double.

## HOSTILE ARTILLERY.

The enemy fired heavily on to SAILLY, the CHATEAU and West side of Village from 11-45 A.M. to 12-15 P.M. and from 10-5 P.M. to 10-45 P.M. Our retaliation silenced the enemy's guns on each occasion.

## INTELLIGENCE.

An S.O.S. Signal was sent up on the left of the Division on our right at about 10-15 P.M.: all was quiet on our front except for the shelling.

The enemy appears to have a T sap about U 8 a 10.4. where a sniper is posted: this point is under 60 yards from our trenches.

During night opposite left Battalion enemy sent up lights from his reserve trenches, indicating that front line is not held in strength in this sector.

*Movements.* Very little movement behind the enemy's line reported. Trains were seen but appeared to be further off than usual.

Captain,

Intellifence Officer, 1st Guards Bde.,

SECRET.

Copy No 5

## WARNING ORDER.

### GUARDS DIVISION ORDER NO.104.

1. Para. 15 Guards Division Order No. 103 is cancelled.

2. The Division will commence to take over a portion of the line on the 9th instant, relief to be completed by the 11th instant.

ACKNOWLEDGE.

Seymour
Captain,
General Staff, Guards Division.

2nd January 1916.

Issued to Signals at 11 pm.

Copy No. 1 General Staff.
2 "Q"
3 G.D.A.
4 C.R.E.
5 1st Guards Brigade.
6 2nd Guards Brigade.
7 3rd Guards Brigade.
8 Pioneer Battalion.
9 Divnl. Signals.
10 A.D.M.S.
11 A.D.V.S.
12 A.P.M.
13 Divnl. Train.
14 Senior Supply Officer.
15 O.C., Supply Column.
16 D.A.D.O.S.
17 War Diary.

S E C R E T.　　　　　　　　　　　　　　　　　　　　　Copy No. 11.

293/A

## WARNING ORDER

### 1st Guards Brigade Order No. 96.

3rd January 1917.

1.   The Division is ordered to begin to take over a portion of the line on the 9th inst., relief to be complete by 11th inst.,

ACKNOWLEDGE.

Captain,

Brigade Major, 1st Guards Brigade.

Issued to Signals at 2 P.M.

Copy No. 1 2nd Grenadier Gds.,  　　No. 7 Bde. Supply Officer.
         2 2nd Coldstream Gds.,  　　　  8 Bde. Transport Officer.
         3 3rd Coldstream Gds.,  　　　  9 O.C., Signals.
         4 1st Irish Gds.,        　　　 10, 11 & 12 Retained.
         5 Bde. Machine Gun Coy.
         6 1st Gds. T.M. Battery.

## HANDING OVER NOTES.

Our front line lies on the forward slope of the high ground East of SAILLY SAILLISEL. The German front line varies in distance from 40 to 350 yards from our own line and is nowhere on higher ground than our own. The enemy does very little sniping either by day or by night, and the two saps opposite the Right Company of the Left Battalion although only 40 yards away appear unoccupied by day. Apparently the enemy is as busy as we are baling out and trying to make some sort of line.

Our own front line is not continuous but it is possible to visit the line held by the Left Front Company of the Right Battalion and the Right Front Company of the Left Battalion by day. There is a gap of 30 yards between the two Battalions.

As the front line is only just on the forward slope it is possible to get quite close to it without being observed by the enemy and therefore the lack of communication trenches matters less than would otherwise be the case.

There is a support trench in each Battalion Area which accommodates 1 Company of each Battalion in the line. This trench is continuous in each Battalion Area, but not between the two Battalions, where there is no trench for nearly 400 yards. Similarly there are even larger gaps between our support line and that of the Brigades on our right and left.

From the support line of the Right Battalion the ground slopes down to the front line but it is possible to get to this support line over the top without being seen.

The support line of the Left Battalion is however, lower than the front line and cannot be seen by the enemy. The enemy can observe the approach to this support line but do not interfere with individuals who pass up and down to it freely all day.

- 2 -

Communication trenches are practically non-existant except for two short ones from the support to the front line in each Battalion area. These are being improved slowly and the Pioneers are digging a new one from the Left Support Company to the CHATEAU. Communication to the CHATEAU by day is by a line of duck-boards running along the N. side of the COMBLES Valley. Another line of duck-boards runs by MOUCHOIR COPSE to the CHATEAU but this is in view from LE TRANSLOY and must not be used by day.

The Advanced Brigade Dump is at the CHATEAU, which pack animals and carrying parties can reach by day. The main Dump is at HAIE Wood where wagons unload and where the DECAUVILLE Railway ends.

Rations are brought up by rail to COMBLES (Western edge of Village), where they are met by pack animals and delivered to the Battalion in COMBLES the day before it is due to go into the trenches.

Pack animals are kept in COMBLES and are allotted by Brigade H.Q., daily for distributing rations and taking stores and material up to the line. Pack animals are supplemented by 5 extra horses from each Battalion in the Group which also remain in COMBLES.

Two Companies are used each morning from the COMBLES Battalion for taking up stores and material to CHATEAU Dump.

Work is being carried out as follows :-

<u>Front Battn's.</u> (a) Maintenance of existing trenches.

            (b) Extension of support line inwards so as to meet and become continuous.

            (c) Wiring of all lines.

<u>The R.E.</u> - are employed on 5 strong points sited with a view to defending our right flank. Three of these are finished i.e. SAILLY in Right Battalion Support Line garrisoned by Right Battalion - SOUTH COPSE garrisoned by COMBLES Battalion and COMBLES at

- 3 -

A Tunnelling Company is making accommodation for another Company at HAIE Wood and is improving the accommodation at the QUARRY.

The Pioneers are digging a communication trench from Left Support Company H.Q., U.2.c.5.8. to the CHATEAU along the Western outskirts of SAILLY SAILLISEL.

There is one good Observation Post in each Battalion Area.

The Artillery have a Liaison Officer at each Battalion H.Q., by night. By day these Officers are supposed to be in their O.P's. but they are short of these.

Areas chiefly shelled are :-
    SAILLY Church -
    PERONNE - BAPAUME Road -
    QUARRY -
    Reserve Line Left Battalion -
    COMBLES Cemetery.

Captain,

31st Dec: 1916.      Brigade Major, 1st Guards Brigade.

SECRET.                                              1st G.B. No. 801.

2nd Bn. Grenadier Guards.    3rd Bn. Coldstream Guards.
1st Bn. Coldstream Guards.   1st Bn. Irish Guards.
2nd Bn. Coldstream Guards.   2nd Bn. Irish Guards.

## AMENDED INSTRUCTIONS NO. 1 FOR RIGHT GROUP.

Subject :- RELIEFS.

1. Trench Roster previously issued still stands good.

2. (a) On Decr. 28th and 29th no troops of Battn's. going into the line will pass BOIS de HAIE before 4 P.M. or after 5-30 P.M.

   (b) On and after Decr. 30th no troops of Battn's. going into the line will pass HAIE WOOD before 5-30 P.M.

3. (a) A Train for Battn's. coming out of the line and moving to Camps 108 or 15 is timed to leave TRONES WOOD Siding for PLATEAU Siding not later than 3 A.M. on the night of their relief. This Train will be drawn up in the Station and troops may embark on arrival at the Siding.

   (b) A Soup Kitchen is established at TRONES WOOD Siding.

   (c) Two Horse Ambulances will meet this Train to convey bad cases from the PLATEAU to Camp.

4. Battn's. coming out of the line and moving to MALTZHORN Camp will move by march route.

5. A Train will leave PLATEAU Siding for TRONES WOOD Siding at 6 P.M. on the day on which any Battalion has to move from Camps 15 or 108 to the COMBLES Area.

6. A Battalion moving into the COMBLES Area from MALTZHORN Camp will move by march route and will not move from Camp before 2 P.M. on Decr. 28th and 29th or before 4 P.M. on and after Decr. 30th.

7. All movement in and out of Camps or trenches will be by platoons in file at 100 yards interval. Troops, transport and pack animals must keep as far as possible to the right of the road.

8. Completion of all movements will be wired by means of XIV Corps Code 'A' to Right Group H.Q., as soon as possible after movement is complete.
   Casualties or any difficulties occurring during the relief should be reported at the same time.

9. Billeting parties will always be sent in advance to take over Camps and Bivouacs.

10. Battalions moving into the line will always send in advance at least 1 N.C.O. per Company and per Battn., H.Q., to take over Stores, etc.,

11. Gum boots will be drawn and handed back into Store as at present. Not more than 200 pairs can be drawn by any one Battn.,

12. Battn's. moving into the COMBLES Area will take up rations for that day and the following day. Rations for the 48 hours for which Battn's. are in the line will be sent up by rail to COMBLES on the day on which Battn's. move into the COMBLES Area. These rations will be met by Pack Animals and delivered to Battn. H.Q. in COMBLES under Brigade arrangements.

13. The Soup Kitchen is on the LEUZE WOOD Road.

27/12/1916.                            Captain,
                         Brigade Major, 1st Guards Brigade.

SECRET.                                         1st G.B. No.801/2.

2nd Bn. Grenadier Guards.      1st Bn. Irish Guards.
1st Bn. Coldstream Guards.     2nd Bn. Irish Guards.
2nd Bn. Coldstream Guards.     75th Field Coy., R.E.
3rd Bn. Coldstream Guards.

## AMENDED INSTRUCTIONS NO.2 FOR RIGHT GROUP.

Subject :- WORK.

1. Battn's. in the line will carry out work in order of importance as follows :-

    (a) Maintenance and revetting and boarding of existing trenches and the construction of fire steps.

    (b) Extension of the Support Line in Right and Left Battn. Areas inwards so as to become one continuous line throughout the Group Sector.

    (c) Wiring of Front and Support Lines. Each Company to put out at least 3 coils of wire during the 24 hours.
    In the Support and Reserve Lines gaps will be left in the wire so that a counter attack can be delivered at once. Gaps must not be visible to the enemy and must be known to Support Reserve Coy's.
    Wiring of unguarded gaps in the Trench Line will be attended to first.
    The number of coils of wire put out will be reported daily in the Intelligence Summary.

2. Sapping Platoons do not go into the Line with their Battn's. but are employed under 75th Coy., R.E. All these are employed as follows :-

    1 platoon-communication trench from right Battn. Support line to front line.

    1 platoon-communication trench from left Battn. support line to front line.

    1 platoon-SAILLY and CUSHY Strong Point.

    1 platoon-CHATEAU and SOUTH COPSE Strong Point.

    1 platoon-upkeep of duck-boards; improvement of Intermediate Line.

    1 platoon-COMBLES Trench and neighbouring accommodation.

### PIONEERS.

3. One Company 4th Bn. Coldstream Guards is employed on digging a communication trench from the Support Company H.Q., Left Battn. (U.8.c.6.8) to the CHATEAU, along the Western edge of SAILLY SAILLISEL Village.

4. Working parties East of COMBLES will not move about in larger parties than 25.

5/

5.      Battn's. in the COMBLES Area will be required to find about 2 Coy's. for work while in the COMBLES Area. Four Cookers with horses are at the disposal of the Battn. in the COMBLES Area for its dinners and teas on the day it goes into the line. These can go up as far as HAIE Wood, if required.

6.      R.E. Material and Stores are delivered by Group H.Q., to the Advanced Dump at the CHATEAU for Battn's. in the line.

## SALVAGE.

7.      Officers in charge of Working and Carrying parties are responsible for bringing back as much Salvage as possible and dumping it at HAIE Wood. O.C's Battn's. in the line are responsible for making full use of any Working or Carrying parties in their neighbourhood to bring back Salvage collected by their Battalions.

28th Dec: 1916.

Captain,
Brigade Major, 1st Guards Brigade.

SECRET.                                                Copy No ... 5.

(296)

## GUARDS DIVISION ORDER NO. 105.

1.     The 3rd Guards Brigade will move one Battalion from BILLON CAMPS to MAUREPAS on January 11th. Not to move from Camp before 1 p.m.

   Route. MARICOURT - HARDECOURT.

2.     An interval of 200 yards between Companies will be maintained.

3.     A billeting party from the above Battalion should report to the Camp Commandant, MAUREPAS, on January 10th, to take over the accommodation vacated that day by the 2nd Bn. Irish Guards. This accommodation will not be occupied during the night of January 10th/11th.

4.     After arrival in the MAUREPAS Area this Battalion will be required for work under the orders of the Division.

ACKNOWLEDGE.

8th January 1917.

Captain, for
General Staff. Guards Divn.

Issued to Signals at 8 p.m.

Copy No. 1  General Staff.           12  A.P.M.
        2  "Q".                      13  Divnl. Train.
        3  G.D.A.                    14  Senior Supply Officer.
        4  C.R.E.                    15  O.C. Supply Column.
        5  1st Guards Brigade.       16  D.A.D.O.S.
        6  2nd Guards Brigade.       17  Sanitary Section.
        7  3rd Guards Brigade.       18  20th Division.
        8  Pioneer Battalion.        19  40th Division.
        9  Signals.                  20  Camp Comdt. MAUREPAS.
       10  A.D.M.S.                  21  XIV Corps.
       11  A.D.V.S.                  22  War Diary.

SECRET.                                            Copy No ...3...

## AMENDMENT TO GUARDS DIVISION ORDER NO. 104.

1. Provisional March Table attached to Guards Division Order No. 104 is cancelled and the attached substituted.

2. After arrival in the MAUREPAS and BILLON FARM Areas, 2nd and 3rd Guards Brigades will come under orders of G.O.C. 8th Division until 10 a.m. January 11th.

3. The front to be held by Guards Division will be covered by XV Corps Artillery until the morning of January 14th, when relief of XV Corps by XIV Corps Artillery will be complete.

4. All trench stores, Secret trench maps, air photographs and Defence Schemes will be taken over and receipts given.

5. The working parties now being found by 3rd Guards Brigade at MERICOURT will be taken over by 1st Guards Brigade in time to start work on the morning of January 10th.

The parties now being found by 3rd Guards Brigade at the PLATEAU will be similarly taken over by 1st Guards Brigade on morning of January 11th.

1st Guards Brigade will continue to find these fatigues until about 16th instant, when all except fatigue parties Nos. IV, V, VI, and IX, referred to in this office No.2502/6/G of 29th ult. will be taken over by 17th Division.

Care must be taken that there is no hiatus in the work.

6. Divisional Headquarters will close at CORBIE and open at MAUREPAS at 10 a.m. on January 11th, at which hour G.O.C. Guards Division will take over command from G.O.C. 8th Division.

ACKNOWLEDGE.

Captain, for
General Staff, Guards Divn.

7th January 1917.

Issued to Signals at 4 p.m.

| Copy No. | | |
|---|---|---|
| 1 | General Staff. | 13 Divnl. Train. |
| 2 | "Q". | 14 Senior Supply Officer. |
| 3 | G.D.A. | 15 O.C. Supply Column. |
| 4 | C.R.E. | 16 D.A.D.O.S. |
| 5 | 1st Guards Brigade. | 17 Sanitary Section. |
| 6 | 2nd Guards Brigade. | 18 8th Division. |
| 7 | 3rd Guards Brigade. | 19 20th Division. |
| 8 | Pioneer Battalion. | 20 40th Division. |
| 9 | Signals. | 21 Camp Commandant. |
| 10 | A.D.M.S. | 22 XIV Corps. |
| | | 23 Town Major, CORBIE. |

MARCH TABLE TO BE ATTACHED TO GUARDS DIVISION ORDER NO. 104.
*************************************************************

| DATE. | UNIT. | FROM. | TO. | ROUTE. | REMARKS. |
|---|---|---|---|---|---|
| Jan.9th. | 2nd Guards Bde. (4 Battalions, M.G.Coy. & T.M.Batt.) | CORBIE. | MAUREPAS & BILLON Camps. | CORBIE - BRAY Road - thence via BRONFAY, MARICOURT & HARDECOURT. | 2 Bns. to MAUREPAS. 2 Bns. to BILLON Camp. Busses for 2 Bns. and M.G.Coy. have been arranged for by "Q", by whom details as to time etc. will be issued. |
|  | 2nd Guards Bde. | MAUREPAS and BILLON Camps. | LINE. | Any. | Relieving 23rd Inf. Bde. Arrangements direct with 23rd Inf.Bde. To be clear of BILLON Camps by 12 noon. |
|  | 3rd Guards Bde. | VILLE, MERICOURT & MEAULTE. | BILLON Camps (107 and 16). | MEAULTE - CARGAILLOT FM.- road junction L.15.b.3.8 - BRONFAY FARM. | Not to arrive at BILLON Camps before 12 noon. 3rd Guards Bde. will reconnoitre a Brigade H.Q. at F.24.c.5.0 |
| Jan.10th. | 1 Bn. 1st Guards Bde. | SANDPITS. | VILLE or MERICOURT. | Main MEAULTE - MERICOURT Road. | Not to move before 1 p.m. |
|  | 1 Bn. 1st Guards Bde. | MEAULTE. | VILLE or MERICOURT. | --do-- | --do-- |
|  | 1st Gds.Bde. M.G.Coy. | MEAULTE. | TREUX. | --do-- | Not to move before 1 p.m. |
|  | 1st Gds.Bde.H.Q. | --do-- | VILLE. | --do-- | --do-- |
| Jan.11th. | Guards Division H.Q. | CORBIE. | MAUREPAS. | CORBIE - BRAY - MARICOURT. |  |

1. All movement of troops east of and including MEAULTE will be by Companies in file at 200 yards interval between Coys. and 500 yards between Battalions.
2. Troops moving on MARICOURT - BRAY Road will do so at intervals of 500 yards between Companies.

SECRET.　　　　　　　　　　　　　　　　　　　Copy No. 5

## WARNING ORDER (2)
## GUARDS DIVISION ORDER NO.104.

1.　　The Division (less Artillery) will relieve a portion of the 8th Division in the line, relief to be completed by 8 a.m. on the 11th January.

2.　　The frontage to be taken over by the Division is from U.20.b.3.2 to U.26.c.7.3.

3.　　This front will be held by two battalions with two battalions in Support, in the area PRIEZ FARM MAUREPAS VALLEY.

4.　　The 2nd Guards Brigade will relieve the 23rd Infantry Brigade in the line on the night 10th/11th January. Details of relief to be arranged between G.Os.C. concerned.

5.　　The 3rd Guards Brigade will be in Support with two battalions MAUREPAS area and two battalions BILLON FARM.

6.　　The 1st Guards Brigade will be in reserve with two battalions MEAULTE, one battalion and Brigade Hd.Qrs. at VILLE, one battalion at MERICOURT and M.G.Coy and T.M.Battery at TREUX.

7.　　Movements in connection with the relief are shown in the attached table.

8.　　C.R.E. will arrange with C.R.E., 8th Division details of relief of R.E. and Pioneer Battalion.

　　A.D.M.S. will arrange with A.D.M.S., 8th Division details of relief of Medical Units.

　　Arrangements to be submitted to this office.

ACKNOWLEDGE.

　　　　　　　　　　　　　　　　　　　　　　K.F.Hambro
　　　　　　　　　　　　　　　　　　　　　　Captain,
　　　　　　　　　　　　　　　　　　　　for Lieut-Colonel,
6th January 1917.　　　　　　General Staff, Guards Division.
Issued to Signals at 8 p.m.

| Copy No.1 General Staff. | 9. Signals. | 17 Sanitary Secn. |
| 2 "Q" | 10 A.D.M.S. | 18 8th Division. |
| 3 G.D.A. | 11 A.D.V.S. | 19 20th Division. |
| 4 C.R.E. | 12 A.P.M. | 20 XIV Corps. |
| 5 1st Guards Bde. | 13 Divnl.Train. | 21 War Diary. |
| 6 2nd Guards Bde. | 14 S.S.O. | |
| 7 3rd Guards Bde. | 15 O.C. Supply Col. | |
| 8 Pioneer Battn. | 16 D.A.D.O.S. | |

## PROVISIONAL MARCH TABLE.

| Date. | Unit. | | From. | To. | Remarks. |
|---|---|---|---|---|---|
| Jan.9th. | 2nd Guards Bde. Group. | by road. | CORBIE. | BILLON FARM MAUREPAS area. | Busses will be arranged if possible for troops going to MAUREPAS. |
| Jan.10th. | 2nd Guards Bde. Group. | —do— | MAUREPAS BILLON FARM area. | LINE. | Relief of 23rd Inf.Bde. |
| | 3rd Guards Bde. Group. | —do— | VILLE MERICOURT MEAULTE | BILLON FARM. | Not to arrive before 12 noon. |
| | Brigade Hd.Qrs. 1st Guards Bde. 1 battalion 1st Guards Bde. | —do— | MEAULTE. | VILLE. | Not to move before 1 pm. |
| | M.G.Coy & T.M.Baty. 1 battalion 1st Guards Bde. | —do— | SANDPITS camp. | MERICOURT. | Not to move before 1 pm. |

SECRET.                                                     Copy No. 17

297
          1st Guards Brigade order No. 96.
          ─────────────────────────────────
                                              8th January 1917.

1.      From January 10th the 1st Guards Brigade will be in reserve
with two battalions at MEAULTE, one battalion and Brigade Headquarters at VILLE, one battalion at MERICOURT, Bde Machine Gun Coy.
and Trench Mortar Battery at TREUX.

2.      Movements will take place in accordance with attached
March Table.

3.      Billeting parties will report to the Town Majors of VILLE,
MERICOURT and TREUX at least four hours before their Units are
due to arrive.

4.      1st Line Transport will move in rear of Units.

5.      Fatigue Roster issued under No. B.M.329 of the 3rd instant.
except for daily fatigues will hold good.

   (a) Fatigue will be taken over by the 2nd Bn Grenadier Guards.
   (b) Fatigue will be taken over by the 3rd Bn Coldstream Guards.

        Arrangements will be made direct between Battalions so that
work is started by these Units on the morning of the 10th without
interruption.


        ACKNOWLEDGE.              H.B./Burn         Captain.
        ─────────────                               ───────
                                   Brigade Major, 1st Guards Brigade.
                                   ─────────────────────────────────

Issued through signals at :- 8 a.m.

Copy No 1. 2/Gren. Gds.          10. No 4 Field Ambulance.
       2. 2/Cold. Gds.           11. 75th Field Coy. R.E.
       3. 3/Cold. Gds.           12. Bde. Transport Officer.
       4. 1/Irish Gds.           13. Bde. Supply Officer.
       5. Bde.M.G.Coy.           14. Town Major.
       6. Bde.T.M.Battery        15. Staff Captain.
       7. Guards Divn.           16. O.C. Signals.
       8. 2nd Guards Bde.        17 - 21. Retained.
       9. 3rd Guards Bde.

MARCH TABLE.

| Date. | UNIT. | From. | To. | Route. | Remarks. |
|---|---|---|---|---|---|
| Jan. 10th. | Bde. H.Q. by road. | MEAULTE. | VILLE. | direct. | To be clear of road junction E 22 b 4.9 by 4 p.m. |
| Jan. 10th. | 2/Cold. Gds. by road. | MEAULTE. | VILLE. | direct. | Battalion to move through MEAULTE in file. 500 yards between Coys. to be clear of road junction E 22 b 4.9 by 3.30 p.m. |
| Jan. 10th. | 1/Irish Gds. by road. | SANDPITS CAMP. | MERICOURT. | VILLE - TREUX - MERICOURT. | Battalion to move through MEAULTE in file. 500 yards between Coys. Battn. to be clear of road junction E 22 b 4.9 by 2 p.m. |
| Jan. 10th. | Bde.M.G.Coy. by road. | MEAULTE. | TREUX. | VILLE - TREUX. | To be clear of road junction E 22 b 4.9 by 2.30 p.m. |

SECRET.                                                   Copy No. 11

## 1st Guards Brigade Order No 97.

9th January 1917.

1.  The following alteration in billets will take place tomorrow
10th instant other than those already arranged for in Brigade Order
No 96 of the 8th instant.

2.  The 2nd Bn Grenadier Guards will vacate their present billets
in MEAULTE and take over those of 1st Bn Grenadier Guards. Area
"A" MEAULTE.

3.  Details to be arranged direct with 1st Bn Grenadier Guards.

4.  Companies will move at not less than 10 minute intervals in
order to avoid any congestion of traffic.

5.  Move to be complete by 1 p.m.

6.  Units of this Bde will adjust their Billets and boards will be
set up showing clearly the Boundaries of each Unit's Area in col-
laboration with the Town Major's of the Villages concerned.

This work to be done by advanced billeting parties and completed by 2 p.m. tomorrow the 10th instant.

A report to this effect to reach this Office by 6 p.m.

7.  Brigade Headquarters will close at MEAULTE at 3 p.m. and
re-open at VILLE at the same hour Jany. 10th.

ACKNOWLEDGE.

                                                    Captain.
                                    a/Brigade Major, 1st Guards Brigade.

Issued through Signals at 3.30 p.m.

Copy No 1.   2nd Bn Grenadier Guards.
       2.   2nd Bn Coldstream Guards.
       3.   3rd Bn Coldstream Guards.
       4.   1st Bn Irish Guards.
       5.   Bde. Machine Gun Coy.
       6.   Guards Division.
       7.   3rd Guards Brigade.
       8.   Town Major, MEAULTE.
       9.   Staff Captain.
      10.)
      11.)  Retained.
      12.)

1st G.B. No.90/1.

2nd Bn. Grenadier Guards.
3rd Bn. Coldstream Guards.
4th Bn. Coldstream Guards.
1st Bn. Irish Guards.

Reference 1st Guards Brigade Order No.90/1. Table "C" is cancelled and following is substituted :-

| Fatigue No. | Strength of party | Report to. | Work. | Billetted & rationed by. | Remarks. |
|---|---|---|---|---|---|
| 1. | 1 Sgt. 30 O.R. | R.E. Office | Cutting trees for fuel supply | M.T.M.T.D. | 7 a.m. daily. |
| 2. | 1 N.C.O. 8 O.R. | R.T.O. Office WITRY. | Unloading fuel train Cartng. at WITRY. | Mt. Trix at Camp Dorengeant & Refilling joint. | |
| 3. | 10 O.R. | O.C. 76th R.E. Road construction, Guards Div. Group. | Road construction, Guards Div. Group. | Billetted by 76th R.E. Rationed by Bn. finding fatigue. | |

Battalions will find these fatigues as follows :-

2nd Cold. Gds. till 29th incl.
2nd Gren. Gds. from 30th to 2nd incl.
3rd Cold. Gds. from 3rd to 6th incl.
1st Irish Gds. from 7th to 10th incl.

Arrangements will be made between Battalions for taking over these fatigues so that there will be no break in the work.

In addition, a Guard will be found by Battalions for Brigade H.Q. as follows :-

2nd Cold. Gds. till 1 p.m. 30th.
2nd Gren. Gds. from 30th to 4.7.m. Feb. 3rd.
3rd Cold. Gds. " " " 3rd " " 7th.
1st Irish Gds. " " " 7th " " 11th.

Brigade Major, 1st Guards Brigade.

28th January 1917.

2nd Grenadier Gds.
2nd Coldstream Gds.
3rd Coldstream Gds.
1st Irish Gds.
1st Guards M.G.Coy.

1st Guards Bde. No. 1225.

1. Reference O.D. No. 2660/3, para. 4, the "Normal attack formation" therein mentioned will be as outlined on attached paper. It must be clearly understood that this formation may have to be modified to suit special circumstances.

2. With reference to para. 5, it is hoped to obtain a supply of large scale maps showing well-established systems of enemy trenches. These maps, when received, will be issued, and attack schemes on them will be set for Battalions.

3. Fourth Army G.S. 360 should be carefully studied.

17th January 1917.

Captain,
Brigade Major, 1st Guards Brigade.

# NORMAL ATTACK FORMATION.

### (A). A Battalion in attack.

3 Companies front line
1 in Reserve.

Each of the leading 3 Companies will be distributed in depth as shown below :-

|  | ½ Platoon. | ½ Platoon. |  |
|---|---|---|---|
| 1st Wave |  |  | ........... |
| 2nd Wave. | { ½ Platoon. } | { ½ Platoon. } | 25 yards. |
|  |  |  | ........... |
| 3rd Wave. | 1 Platoon. |  | 25 yards. |
|  |  |  | ........... |
| 4th Wave. | 1 Platoon. |  | 25 yards. |
|  |  |  | ........... |

The fourth wave may be in small columns.

The frontage of the battalion will be such as to admit of the men being in extended order at from 3 to 5 paces extension. A normal frontage for a battalion would be about 400 yards.

The Reserve Company will follow the 3 leading Companies in line of platoon columns at a distance of 25 to 50 yards.

"Moppers up" will be distributed as required according to the number of objectives. They will normally be found from one battalion of the Brigade, which will be split up for the purpose.(See below).

"Moppers up" will be 10 yards in rear of the wave they are detailed to follow.

The 2 leading platoons of each Company will normally be formed up for the attack in our front line trench.

The 2 rear platoons will be formed up in a support trench in rear.

A third trench will be used to accomodate the Reserve Company.

The leading wave, reinforced as required, will normally advance to the first objective, ( i.e. will not halt on a preliminary objective and let the succeeding waves pass through it); but this latter method of waves passing through one another should be practised when the normal procedure has been thoroughly mastered.

### (B). The Brigade in attack.

Normal distribution.

2 Battalions front line. (distributed as above).
1 Battalion in Reserve.
1 Battalion providing all clearing up parties, carrying parties, and if necessary, parties for consolidation of special points.

If the frontage is too great for 2 Battalions, the reserve will be disponsed with, and the attack made with 3 Battalions in line.

The Reserve Battalion is normally for use as its names indicates, but may be required for a definite object, e.g. the assault of an objective beyond that allotted to the front line battalions.

S E C R E T.                                              G.D. No. 2660/11.

G.R.E.
1st Guards Brigade.
2nd Guards Brigade.
3rd Guards Brigade.
————————

1.  The Army Commander has laid down the necessity of
practising a drill attack formation, and has pointed out
that a frontage of 400 yards may be considered as suitable
for a Battalion in an attack on a simple system of trenches
(two lines of trenches not more than 100 yards apart).  This
allows 2 men per yard of front attacked including "cleaners up"
and "carriers".  These figures will form the basis on which a
drill attack formation will be worked out.

2.  The object of this drill attack is to instil a thorough
knowledge of the duties of the various commanders and the tasks
of the several portions of the attacking force, also the duties
of specialists and how they can best cooperate in the attack.

3.  In action against the enemy it should not prove difficult
to adapt the normal attack formation to one fitted to the
particular conditions that have to be faced.  In this regard the
various factors affecting formations are very clearly
summarised in Fourth Army G.S.380 of 1st December (G.D.No. 2618/G
of 12th December 1916) which will bear careful study.

4.  When a Brigade is in Corps Reserve the Major-General
wishes Battalions to practise a normal attack formation as
above outlined.

   Where it is not possible to practise the Battalion attack
on the ground as a whole, a well known system of enemy trenches
should be selected and the attack worked out in detail on the map,
Company or platoon attacks on the ground being subsequently
carried out in connection with the scheme.

/2.

2.

5. In working out these attacks the Major-General lays stress on the following points:-

    (a) The writing of the necessary and detailed attack orders, both by Battalion, Company, and Platoon Commanders and by O.C. Machine Gun Company.

    (b) The tactical use of ground.

    (c) The allotment of definite tasks to units and to various specialists.

    (d) The details of equipment to be carried.

    (e) Arrangements for "cleaning up" of enemy trenches.

    (f) The position in the attacking force of Lewis guns and their employment on reaching the objective.

    (g) Arrangements for consolidation of the captured position.

    (h) Arrangements for communication with aircraft.

6. As laid down in Fourth Army S.S.400 (G.D.No.2050/G of 21st December 1916) the platoon will be the fighting unit, trained and led by its commander.

    Each platoon will fulfil the following conditions:-

    A. Each man must be able to throw a bomb.

    B. Each platoon must have its own trained bombing section.

    C. 50% must be trained to use the Mills adapter.

    D. Some men must be able to use the rifle grenade.

7. The rifle and bayonet are still the primary infantry weapons in the attack.

    The employment of covering fire, both from rifles and machine guns, must be encouraged.

8. The Major-General wishes Brigadiers to hold Conferences both before and after attack practises at which all officers of a Battalion should be present.

    At these Conferences all details of the attack should be dealt with.

(sd) C.P.HEYWOOD,
Lieut-Colonel,
General Staff, Guards Divn.

15th January 1917.

SECRET.

1st Guards Bde. No. 1288.

2nd Grenadier Gds.
2nd Coldstream Gds.
3rd Coldstream Gds.
1st Irish Gds.
1st Guards M.G.Coy.
1st Guards T.M. Battery.

As a result of a Conference held at Division Hd.Qrs. on January 18th, the following Orders are issued:-

(I).    The pamphlet "Training for Divisions for Offensive Action" has been issued not as a guide but as an order. It must be studied and followed in the same manner as Field Service Regulations or the Infantry Training Manual, and all Officers <u>must thoroughly know its contents.</u>
    Stress is laid on page 17, para. 5, which refers to the necessity of organising the platoon as a self-contained unit.

(II)    Page 30 - Distinguishing marks to denote Battalions, Companies, and Specialists.
    These are to be adopted as soon as issued, which will be at an early date.
    The Distinguishing marks to be worn by Battalions have been laid down in G.S. No. 1057/2/A of 10/1/17, issued under this Office No. 980 of 10/1/17.
    As regards Specialists,
    Scouts, Runners, Regimental and Company Signallers, will wear distinguishing marks as soon as issued.
    Badges for Carrying Parties and Mopping up Parties will be kept at Brigade Hd.Qrs. and issued to Battalions shortly before an operation.
    Battalion and Company Signallers will <u>not</u> wear the blue and white band.

(III)   As regards the three forms of attack for which training is necessary, page 7, para. 2. All training in the Brigade will for the present be devoted to training for the initial attack against a well organised and long-established line of trenches.

(IV)    It is necessary, since Company and Platoon Commanders have little previous instruction in how to train their units, that Commanding Officers should ensure that every Commander, before going out on a day's training, have a definite programme for the day's training, thought out in detail overnight.

(V)     With reference to "4th Army Standing Orders on Defence against Gas" issued in the pamphlet form S.S.443, one to each Battalion Hd.Qrs. and one per Company. Commanding Officers will ensure that these orders are familiar to all ranks, and that when in the line all precautions to be taken in case of a gas alert are strictly adhered to.

ACKNOWLEDGE.

                                            H.W.O'Brien   Captain,
19th January 1917.                    Brigade Major, 1st Guards Bde.

SECRET.  802/1                                          Copy No. 5

## GUARDS DIVISION ORDER NO. 106.

1. (a)   3rd Guards Brigade will relieve 2nd Guards Brigade in the line on the nights of 25th/26th and 26th/27th.

   Details of reliefs to be arranged between Brigades concerned.

   (b)   On relief 2nd Guards Brigade will move back into Corps Reserve area (VILLE - TREUX - MERICOURT).

   (c)   1st Guards Brigade will move into the BILLON area (1 Battalion at PRIEZ FARM) and will become Divisional Reserve.

   (d)   55th Field Coy. R.E. will relieve 76th Field Coy. R.E., the latter moving on relief to BRONFAY FARM.

   75th Field Coy. R.E. will move to MAUREPAS.

   Movements will be carried out in accordance with Appendix "A" attached. Detail of routes and times of starting will be issued later.

2.   2nd Guards Brigade will take over all Corps working parties now found by 1st Guards Brigade, arrangements being such that there is no hiatus in the work.

   The relief by 2nd Guards Brigade of the Decauville working party of 400 men, now found by 1st Guards Brigade, will form subject of a separate order.

ACKNOWLEDGE.

                                            (P) H Heywood
                                            Lieut-Colonel,
21st January 1917.                          General Staff. Guards Divn.

Issued to Signals at 12.30 a.m.

Copy No. 1 General Staff.            13 Divnl. Train.
        2 "Q".                       14 Senior Supply Officer.
        3 G.D.A.                     15 O.C. Supply Column.
        4 C.R.E.                     16 D.A.D.O.S.
        5 1st Guards Brigade.        17 20th Division.
        6 2nd Guards Brigade.        18 40th Division.
        7 3rd Guards Brigade.        19 XIV Corps.
        8 Pioneer Battalion.         20 Camp Comdt. MAUREPAS.
        9 Signals.                   21     "       BILLON CAMP.
       10 A.D.M.S.                   22 Town Major VILLE.
       11 A.D.V.S.                   23     "      MERICOURT.
       12 A.P.M.                     24 War Diary.

MOVEMENTS OF BATTALIONS ETC. DURING RELIEF.   APPENDIX "A".

| DATE. | UNIT. | FROM. | TO. | REMARKS. |
|---|---|---|---|---|
| Jan.24th | 2nd Irish Guards | MAUREPAS | VILLE | By bus or rail. |
| | 1st Welsh Guards | BILLON CAMP | MAUREPAS | |
| | 3rd Gds.Bde.M.G.Co. and Light T.M.Batt. | BILLON CAMP | MAUREPAS | |
| | 2nd Coldstream Gds. | VILLE | BILLON FARM | |
| | 1st Coldstream Gds | LINE | VILLE | Taking over billets vacated by 2 Bns. 51st Inf. |
| | 3rd Grenadier Gds. | MAUREPAS | MERICOURT | By bus. |
| | 2nd Gds.Bde.M.G.Co. and Light T.M.Batt. | LINE | MAUREPAS | By bus or rail |
| | 1st Grenadier Gds. | PRIEZ FARM | MAUREPAS | |
| | 1st Welsh Guards. | MAUREPAS | LINE | |
| Jan.25th | 3rd Gds.Bde.M.G.Co. and Light T.M.Batt. | MAUREPAS | LINE | |
| | 4th Grenadier Gds. | BILLON FARM | MAUREPAS | |
| | 2nd Grenadier Gds. | MEAULTE } Billets vacated will be taken over by 2 Bns. 60th Inf. Bde. | PRIEZ FARM | By bus to MAUREPAS. |
| | 3rd Coldstream Gds. | MEAULTE } | BILLON FARM. | |
| | 55th Field Co. R.E. | MAUREPAS. | LINE. | |
| | 76th Field Co. R.E. | LINE | MOLAY FARM | |
| | 75th Field Co. R.E. | MOLAY FARM | MAUREPAS | |

| DATE. | UNIT. | FROM. | TO. | REMARKS |
|---|---|---|---|---|
| Jan. 26th. | 1st Scots Guards | LINE | MAUREPAS | |
| | 2nd Gds.Bde.M.G.Co. and Light T.M.Batt. | MAUREPAS | TREUX | |
| | 2nd Gds.Bde. Hd.Qrs. | LINE | VILLE | |
| | 4th Grenadier Gds. | MAUREPAS | LINE | |
| | 3rd Gds.Bde. Hd.Qrs. | BILLON CAMP | LINE | |
| | 1st Gds.Bde. Hd.Qrs. | VILLE | BILLON CAMP | |
| | 1st Gds.Bde.M.G.Co. and Light T.M.Batt. | TREUX and MEAULTE. | BILLON CAMP. | Camp 10/ |
| Jan. 27th. | 1st Scots Guards | MAUREPAS | MERICOURT | By bus or rail. |
| | 2nd Scots Guards | BILLON CAMP | MAUREPAS | |
| | 1st Irish Guards | MERICOURT | BILLON CAMP | Camp 10/ 2nd S.G. |

APPENDIX "E".

## DISTRIBUTION OF GUARDS BRIGADES ETC.
### ON COMPLETION OF RELIEF.

| BRIGADE IN THE LINE. | DIVISIONAL RESERVE. | CORPS RESERVE. |
|---|---|---|
| 3rd Guards Brigade. | 1st Guards Brigade. | 2nd Guards Brigade. |
| Brigade Headquarters E.4.c.3.9. | Brigade Headquarters BILLON CAMP. | Brigade Headquarters VILLE. |
| 1st Bn. Grenadier Guards MAUREPAS. | 2nd Bn. Grenadier Guards PRIEZ FARM. | 3rd Bn. Grenadier Guards MERICOURT. |
| 4th Bn. Grenadier Guards LINE. | 2nd Bn. Coldstream Guards BILLON CAMP. | 1st Bn. Coldstream Guards VILLE. |
| 2nd Bn. Scots Guards MAUREPAS. | 3rd Bn. Coldstream Guards -do- | 1st Bn. Scots Guards MERICOURT. |
| 1st Bn. Welsh Guards LINE. | 1st Bn. Irish Guards -do- | 2nd Bn. Irish Guards VILLE. |
| M.G.Co. and T.M.Batt. LINE. | M.G.Co. and T.M.Batt. -do- | M.G.Co. and T.M.Batt. TREUX. |
| 55th Field Co. R.E. LINE. | 75th Field Co. R.E. MAUREPAS. | |
| | 76th Field Co. R.E. BETHAY FARM | |

# SECRET

G.D. No.2696/5/G.

"Q".
G.D.A.
C.R.E.
1st Guards Brigade.
2nd Guards Brigade.
3rd Guards Brigade.
Pioneer Battalion.
Signals.
A.D.M.S.
A.D.V.S.
A.P.M.
Divnl. Train.

Senior Supply Officer.
O.C. Supply Column.
D.A.D.O.S.
20th Division.
40th Division.
17th Division.
XIV Corps.
Camp Comdt. MAUREPAS.
  -do-      BILLON CAMP.
Town Major VILLE.
  -do-     MERICOURT.

---

1. That portion of Appendix "A", Guards Division Order No. 106, which refers to movements of 2nd Bn. Irish Guards and 1st Bn. Coldstream Guards is cancelled and the following substituted.

| DATE. | UNIT. | FROM. | TO. |
|---|---|---|---|
| 24th Jan. | 2nd Bn. Irish Guards (less Detachment). | MAUREPAS. | BRIQUETERIE, A.4.b.5.1. |
|  | Detachment, 2nd Bn. Irish Guards. | MAUREPAS. | VILLE. |
| 25th Jan. | 1st Bn. Coldstream Gds. | LINE. | MAUREPAS. |
| 26th Jan. | 1st Bn. Coldstream Gds. | MAUREPAS. | VILLE. |

2. During the process of relief G.Os.C. Guards Brigades will have under their tactical command all Battalions in their respective Brigade areas.

3. March Table, giving routes and times of starting for movements ordered in Guards Division Order No. 106, is attached.

ACKNOWLEDGE.

*CPHeywood*

Lieut-Colonel,
General Staff, Guards Divn.

22nd January 1917.

| DATE. | UNIT. | FROM. | TO. | ROUTE. | REMARKS. |
|---|---|---|---|---|---|
| Jan.24th | 2/Coldstream Guards | VILLE | BILLON CAMP | MORLANCOURT - K.21.b.8.8 - BRAY | To be clear of VILLE by 9 a.m. |
| | 1/Welsh Guards. | BILLON CAMP | MAUREPAS | MARICOURT - HARDECOURT | To clear BILLON CAMP by 8.30 a.m. |
| | 2/Irish Guards (less Detachment) | MAUREPAS | BRIQUETERIE | HARDECOURT - A.17.b and d. | To clear Camp by 9.30 a.m. |
| | Detachment 2/I.G. | MAUREPAS | VILLE | "March to PLATEAU thence by rail" | -do- |
| | 3rd Gds.Bde.M.G.Co. and T.M.Batt. | BILLON CAMP | MAUREPAS | MARICOURT - HARDECOURT | To clear BILLON CAMP by 9 a.m. |
| | 3/Grenadier Guards | MAUREPAS | MERICOURT | March to PLATEAU, thence by road Transport by rail via MARICOURT FRICOURT - MEAULTE. | Bn. to clear Camp by 9.30 a.m. Transport to clear lines by 7.30 a.m. |
| | 4/Grenadier Guards | BILLON CAMP | MAUREPAS | MARICOURT - HARDECOURT | To clear BILLON CAMP by 8.30 a.m. |
| Jan.25th | 2/Grenadier Guards | MEAULTE | PRIEZ FARM | FRICOURT - PERONNE AVENUE - MARICOURT by march route CARGAILLOT Cross roads, L.15.b. | To be clear of MEAULTE by 8 a.m. |
| | 3/Coldstream Guards | MEAULTE | BILLON CAMP | MARICOURT - HARDECOURT | To be clear of MEAULTE by 11 a.m. (Not to move before Noon). |
| | 75th Field Co. R.E. 76th Field Co. R.E. | BRONFAY FARM LINE | MAUREPAS BRONFAY FM. | -do- | Bn to clear Camp by 9.30.a.m. |
| | 1/Coldstream Guards | MAUREPAS | VILLE | March to PLATEAU, thence by rail Transport by road via MARICOURT FRICOURT - MEAULTE. | Transport to clear lines by 7.45 a.m. to march in rear of 2nd Gds.Bde.M.G. Co. transport. |
| Jan.26th | 2ndGds.Bde.H.Q. M.G.Co.& T.M.Batt. | MAUREPAS | TREUX | Personnel march to PLATEAU in rear of 1/Cold:Gds. thence by rail Transport by road via MARICOURT FRICOURT | To clear Camp by 9.45 a.m. Transport to clear lines by 7.30 a.m. |
| | 1st Gds.bde.M.G.Co. and T.M.Batt. | TREUX and MEAULTE. | BILLON. | CARGAILLOT Cross Roads, L.15.b. | To pass CARGAILLOT cross roads by 10 |
| | Hd.Qrs. 1st Gds.Bde. Hd.Qrs. 3rd Gds.Bde. | VILLE BILLON CAMP | BILLON CAMP B.4.c.3.2. | Under Brigade arrangements. -do- | |

| DATE. | UNIT. | FROM. | TO. | ROUTE. | REMARKS. |
|---|---|---|---|---|---|
| | 1st Bn. Scots Guards | MAUREPAS | MERICOURT | March to PLATEAU and thence by rail Transport by road via MARICOURT - FRICOURT. | Bn. to clear Camp by 9.30 a.m. Transport to clear lines by 7.30 a.m. |
| 27th Jan. | 2nd Bn. Scots Guards | BILLON CAMP | MAUREPAS | MARICOURT - HARDECOURT | To clear BILLON CAMP by 8.30 a.m. |
| | 1st Bn. Irish Guards | MERICOURT | BILLON CAMP | J.22.b.7.9 - BRAY | To be clear of MERICOURT by 10 am |

Transport will march with Battalions except where otherwise ordered.

All movement of troops East of and including MEAULTE will be by Companies in file at 200 yards interval between Companies and 500 yards between Battalions.
Troops moving on MARICOURT - BRAY road will do so at intervals of 500 yards between Companies.

Trains leave the PLATEAU on 24th, 25th, 26th and 27th at 11.50 a.m.

\*\*\*\*\*\*\*\*\*\*\*\*\*\*

SECRET.                                                  Copy No. 14.

## 1st Guards Brigade Order No. 98/1.

23rd January 1917.

Reference 1st Guards Brigade Order No. 98 of 21st inst.,

1. Para. 3.

    Corps Working Parties in accordance with attached table "B".

    BRIQUETERIE Fatigue of 8 Officers and 400 O.R. will be relieved in accordance with attached table "C".

    Para. 4.

    Fatigues now found by 3rd Guards Brigade will be taken over in accordance with attached table "D".

2. MARCH TABLE "A"/1 giving routes and times of starting for movements ordered in ~~Guards Division~~ 1st Guards Bde Order No. ~~106~~ 98 is attached.

3. Lorries for Blankets will be arranged and Units will be informed later as to numbers available and times of loading.

4. Brigade H.Q., VILLE, will close at 11 A.M. on 26th inst., and reopen at same hour at BILLON FARM.

5. A Special D.R. will leave Brigade H.Q., for BRIQUETERIE at 7-30 P.M. tonight 23rd inst., calling at 2nd Grenadier Guards Battn., H.Q., MEAULTE on the way to take any Orders Battn's. have for their respective parties at the BRIQUETERIE.

    ACKNOWLEDGE.

                                            H.B. O'Brien
                                            Captain,
                                    Brigade Major, 1st Guards Brigade.

Issued to Signals at 3-30 P.M.
Copy No. 1 2nd Grenadier Gds.      Copy No. 9 3rd Guards Brigade.
         2 2nd Coldstream Gds.              10 Senior Supply Officer.
         3 3rd Coldstream Gds.              11 O.C., No.6 R.E. Park.
         4 1st Irish Gds.                   12 O.C., No.2 Prisoners of War
         5 Bde. M.G. Company.                  Company, MERICOURT.
         6 Bde. Transport Officer.          13 Staff Captain.
         7 Guards Division.                 14 O.C., Signals.
         8 2nd Guards Brigade.              15 Camp Commdt., BILLON FARM.
                                            16 - 20 Retained.
                                    16. T.M. Bty.

MARCH TABLE "A"/1 giving routes, times of starting for movements

Ordered in 1st Guards Brigade Order No.98.

| Date. | Unit. | From. | To. | Route. | Remarks. |
|---|---|---|---|---|---|
| Jan: 24th. | 2/Cold.Gds. | VILLE. | BILLON Camp 16. | MORLANCOURT -K 21 b 8.8. - BRAY. | To be clear of VILLE by 9 A.M. |
| 25th. | 2/Gren.Gds. | MEAULTE. | PRIEZ FARM. | FRICOURT - PERONNE Avenue - MERICOURT by march route. | To be clear of MEAULTE by 8 A.M. |
| | 3/Cold.Gds. | MEAULTE. | BILLON Camp 107. | CARCAILLOT cross - roads L 15 b. | To be clear of MEAULTE by 11 A.M. |
| 26th. | Bde.M.G.Coy. & T.M.Bty. | TREUX. MEAULTE. | BILLON Camp 16. | CARCAILLOT cross - roads L 15 b. | To pass CARCAILLOT cross roads by 10 A.M. |
| | H.Q. 1st Gds.Bde. | VILLE. | BILLON CAMP. | MORLANCOURT -K 24 b 8.8. - BRAY. | Starting Point - Bde. H.Q., 11-30 A.M. |
| 27th. | 1/Irish Gds. | MERICOURT. | BILLON Camp 107. | J 22 b 7.9. - BRAY. | To be clear of MERICOURT by 10 A.M. |

Transport will march with Battalions.
All movements of troops East of and including MEAULTE will be by Companies in file at 200 yards interval between Coy's. and 500 yards between Battalions.
Troops moving on MERICOURT - BRAY Road will do so at intervals of 500 yards between Companies.

Fatigues to be handed over to 2nd Guards Brigade.

TABLE "3".

| Strength of party. | Reporting to. | Work. | Billetted & rationed by. | Unit at present finding. | To be taken over by. | Date. | Time. | Remarks. |
|---|---|---|---|---|---|---|---|---|
| 2 N.C.O's 6 O.R. | Camp Commdt. XIVth Corps H.Q. | Guard for Camp Commdt. prisoners XIV Corps of War. | 3/C.G. H.Q's. | 2/I.G. | 24th. | | Permanent. |
| 1 Offr. 1 Sgt. 115 O.R. | O.C. No.6 R.E. Park MERICOURT. | —do— | O.C. No.6 R.E. Park. | 1/I.G. | 2/I.G. | 25th. | 3 P.M. | Cooker required. Permanent. |
| 1 Sgt. 20 O.R. | O.C. No.2 Prisoners of War Company. | —do— | O.C. No. Prisoners M.G.Coy. of War Company. | Edc. | 2/I.G. | 24th. | — | Permanent. |
| 1 N.C.O. 10 O.R. | Horse Lines 11th Coy. A.S.C.TREUX.Brigade. | To cut wood for finding fatigue. | Battn. | 2/C.G. | 2/I.G. | 24th. | — | Daily.Haversack ration and one cross saw to be taken. |

Relief of Decauville Fatigue at BRIQUETERIE Camp (Map ref. A 4 b 5.2.) TABLE "C".

| Date. | Unit at present finding. | Strength of party. | To be taken over by. | On relief proceed to. | Rejoin Battalion. | | |
|---|---|---|---|---|---|---|---|
| | | | | | Date. | Place. | Remarks. |
| Jan: 24th. | 2/G.G. | 2 Offrs. 100 men. | 2/I.G. | BILLON Camp 16. | 25th. | PRIEZ FARM. | By road. |
| " | 2/C.G. | -do- | -do- | -do- | 24th. | BILLON Camp 16. | By road. |
| " | 3/C.G. | -do- | -do- | -do- | 25th. | BILLON Camp 107. | -do- |
| " | 1/I.G. | 1 Offr. 100 O.R. | -do- | -do- | 27th. | -do- | -do- |

Parties will not work on day of relief.
Arrangements will be made by Camp Commdt. BILLON FARM in conjunction with 2/Cold.Gds.
Camp 16 for accommodation of those parties.
Parties will be rationed direct by Guards Division up to and including the day they rejoin their Battalions.

Medical arrangements at BRIQUETERIE Camp.
M.O. 17th Division Works Battn., visits Camp daily. Surgical Haversack and Medical Companion is held on this Officers charge. Medical Orderly is supplied by No. 9 Field Ambulance and is rationed by the Brigade doing the fatigue.

Fatigue to be taken over from 3rd Guards Brigade.

TABLE "E".

| Fatigue No. | Strength of party. | Report to. | Work. | Billotted & rationed by. | Unit at present finding. | To be taken over by. | Date. | Time. | Remarks. |
|---|---|---|---|---|---|---|---|---|---|
| 1. | 1 Offr. 100 O.R. | 76th Coy. R.E. BRONFAY CAMP. | Camp Improve- ment, Baths etc., | ERONFAY CAMP. | 3/Gds.Bde. | 3/C.G. | 26th. | 9 A.M. | Daily. |
| 2. | 1 N.C.O. 20 O.R. | R.S.O. Office PLATEAU. | Cutting trees for Fuel supply. | Battn. finding fatigue. | 4/G.G. | 2/C.G. | 25th. | 8 A.M. | Daily. |
| 3. | 8 O.R. | R.S.O. Office PLATEAU. | Unloading fuel at PLATEAU. | Train Coy's. Gds.Divn.Train at Camp & Refilling Point. | 1/G.G. | 2/C.G. | 25th. | 8 A.M. | Permanent. |
| 4. | 20 O.R. | O.C. 75th R.E. BOIS MARICOURT A 16.b. | Shed con- struction Gds.Divn. Group. | Billotted by 75th R.E. Rationed by Bn. finding fatigue. | 1/W.G. & 1/G.G. | 2/C.G. | 25th. | 9 A.M. | Permanent. |

S E C R E T.                                              Copy No. 16.

1st Guards Brigade Order No. 98.

21st January 1917.

From 24th to 27th inclusive.

1. The 1st Guards Brigade will move into the BILLON Area (1 Battn. at PRIEZ FARM) to be vacated by 3rd Guards Brigade, and will become Divisional Reserve.

2. Movements will be carried out in accordance with attached TABLE "A".

   Detail of Transport, routes, and times of starting will be issued later.

3. The 2nd Guards Brigade will take over all Corps Working Parties and also the DECAUVILLE working party at BRIQUETERIE of 400 men now found by 1st Guards Brigade.

   These will form the subject of a separate Order.

4. The 1st Guards Brigade will take over fatigues now found by 3rd Guards Brigade, particulars will be issued later.

ACKNOWLEDGE.

H B O Bin'' Captain,

Brigade Major, 1st Guards Brigade.

Issued to Signals at 8-30 P.M.

Copy No. 1 2nd Grenadier Gds.      Copy No. 8 Bde. Transport Officer.
         2 2nd Coldstream Gds.              9 Guards Division.
         3 3rd Coldstream Gds.             10 2nd Guards Brigade.
         4 1st Irish Gds.                  11 3rd Guards Brigade.
         5 Bde. M. G. Company.             12 Staff Captain.
         6 1st Guards T.M.Bty.             13 O.C., Signals.
         7 Bde. Supply Officer.            14, 15 & 16 Retained.

MOVEMENTS OF BATTALIONS ETC., DURING RELIEF.   TABLE "A".

| Date | Unit. | From. | Billets vacated will be taken over by. | To. | To be taken over from. | Remarks. |
|---|---|---|---|---|---|---|
| 24th. | 2/Cold.Gds. | VILLE | | BILLON Camp 16. | 1/Welsh Gds. | By road. |
| 25th. | 2/Gren.Gds. | MEAULTE. | 1 Bn. of 60th Inf.Bde. | PRIEZ FARM. | 1/Gren.Gds. | By bus to MAUREPAS. |
| | 2/G.G. Transport. | " | | B.14.a.2.1. | " | By road. |
| | 3/Cold.Gds. | MEAULTE. | 1 Bn. of 60th Inf.Bde. | DILLON Camp 107. | 4/Gren.Gds. | By road. |
| 26th. | Brigade H.Q., | VILLE. | 2/Gds.Bde.H.Q., | BILLON FARM. | 3/Gds.Bde.H.Q., | By road. |
| | 3do.M.G.Coy. | TREUX. | "  M.G.Coy. | BILLON Camp 16. | "  M.G.Coy. | By road. |
| | Bde.T.M.Bty. | MEAULTE. | "  T.M.Bty. | " | "  T.M.Bty. | By road. |
| 27th. | 1/Irish Gds. | MERICOURT. | | BILLON Camp 107. | 2/Scots Gds. | By road. |

S E C R E T.                                                Copy No. 14.

## 1st Guards Brigade Order No. 99.

28th January 1917.

Battalions in PRIEZ FARM will be relieved in accordance with the following table :-

| | Date. | Unit. | From. | To. | | Date. | Unit. | From. | To. |
|---|---|---|---|---|---|---|---|---|---|
| Battns. to Priez. | 29th. | 3/C.G. | Camp 107. | Priez Farm. | Battns. from Priez. | 29th. | 2/C.G. | Priez Farm. | Camp 107. |
| | 2nd. | 1/I.G. | Camp 107. | -do- | | 2nd. | 3/C.G. | -do- | Camp 107. |
| | 6th. | 2/C.G. | Camp 16. | -do- | | 6th. | 1/I.G. | -do- | Camp 16. |

Routes - MARICOURT - HARDICOURT - MAUREPAS - COMBLES.

Times of starting - Battalion leaving BILLON Farm will be clear of Camp by 9 A.M. Battalion from PRIEZ Farm will move after work on that day.

Transport - Cookers and Water Carts will not be left behind. Transport Lines for Battalion at PRIEZ Farm are situated at S.14.a.2.1.

1. Battalions arriving at PRIEZ Farm will, as soon as possible after arrival, make themselves acquainted with the approaches to the line -
   (a) from MAUREPAS.
   (b) approaches to the Duckboards.
   (c) approaches to Intermediate Line.
   (d) approaches to Reserve Line.

2. Battalions while at PRIEZ Farm are for tactical purposes under the Orders of G.O.C., 3rd Guards Brigade.

3. The relief of 3rd Guards Brigade in the line will take place on the 11th/12th.

ACKNOWLEDGE.

A/O/O'Brien Captain,
Brigade Major, 1st Guards Brigade.

Issued to Signals at 12 noon.

Copy No.1 2nd Grenadier Gds.          Copy No.7 Guards Division.
       2 2nd Coldstream Gds.                   8 3rd Guards Brigade.
       3 3rd Coldstream Gds.                   9 Staff Captain.
       4 1st Irish Gds.                       10 O.C., Signals.
       5 Gds. M.G. Company.                   11 - 14 Retained.
       6 1st Guards T.M. Bty.

S E C R E T.                                              Copy No. 11

Amendment to 1st Guards Brigade Order No. 99.

29th January 1917.

As follows :-

1.      Times of starting - Battalions will be clear of BILLON FARM by 9 A.M.

2.      Battalion at PRIEZ FARM has one Company in Camp H at MAUREPAS RAVINE, map reference B.8.Central.

3.      2 Lorries will be arranged for on days of relief to take the Battalions blankets to and from PRIEZ FARM. The Lorries will call at MAUREPAS RAVINE Camp on the outward and return journey to collect and deposit blankets from the Company in this Camp.
Lorries will be at BILLON Camp entrance at 6 A.M. on relief days.

ACKNOWLEDGE.

H.E. O'Brien             Captain,
Brigade Major, 1st Guards Brigade.

Issued to Signals at 12 noon.

         Copy No. 1  2nd Bn. Grenadier Guards.
                  2  2nd Bn. Coldstream Guards.
                  3  3rd Bn. Coldstream Guards.
                  4  1st Bn. Irish Guards.
                  5  Bde., Machine Gun Company.
                  6  1st Guards T. M. Battery.
                  7  Guards Division.
                  8  3rd Guards Brigade.
                  9  Staff Captain.
                 10  O.C., Signals.
                 11 - 14 Retained.

www.ingramcontent.com/pod-product-compliance
Lightning Source LLC
Chambersburg PA
CBHW081454160426
43193CB00013B/2479